About the Book

Maria Cordero was born in Puerto Rico. When she came to the mainland, she met with prejudice both because she was a woman and because she was from Puerto Rico. Overcoming a language barrier, she earned her doctorate in physiology and went on to become a research scientist and Program Director of the Department of Medical Technology at Louisiana State University, Shreveport.

The story of Maria Cordero Hardy tells of a girl who learned to make choices that helped her achieve the goals she, not others, set.

an American Women in Science biography

Scientist from Puerto Rico, Maria Cordero Hardy

by Mary Ellen Verheyden-Hilliard

drawings by Scarlet Biro

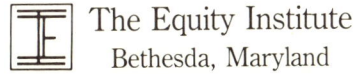

The Equity Institute
Bethesda, Maryland

Copyright © 1985 by The Equity Institute. All rights reserved. No part of this book may be reproduced in any form or by any means, electronic or mechanical, including photo copying, recording or by any information storage and retrieval system, without permission in writing from the Publisher. Published in the United States by The Equity Institute, P.O. Box 30245, Bethesda, Maryland 20814.

This work was developed under a grant from the Women's Educational Equity Act Program, U.S. Department of Education. However, the content does not necessarily reflect the position of that Agency and no official endorsement of these materials should be inferred.

Library of Congress Cataloging in Publication Data

Verheyden-Hilliard, Mary Ellen.
Scientist from Puerto Rico, Maria Cordero Hardy.

(An American women in science biography)

Summary: A biography of a Puerto Rican woman who came to the mainland where she overcame a language barrier, earned a doctorate in physiology, and became a scientist, while fighting prejudice on several levels.

1. Hardy, Maria Cordero—Juvenile literature. 2. Women physiologists—Puerto Rico—Biography—Juvenile literature. 3. Women physiologists—United States—Biography—Juvenile literature. 4. Physiologists—Puerto Rico—Biography—Juvenile literature. 5. Physiologists—United States—Biography—Juvenile literature.
[1. Hardy, Maria Cordero. 2. Women physiologists. 3. Physiologists] I. Biro, Scarlet, ill. II. Title. III. Series: Verheyden-Hilliard, Mary Ellen. American women in science biography.

QP26.H28V47 1985   591.1′092′4 [B] [92]   84-25979
ISBN 0-932469-02-7

Scientist from Puerto Rico,
Maria Cordero Hardy

"Maria. We go now." The laundry women had finished washing the clothes in the river. The clean clothes were carried in bundles on their heads.

"I'm coming." Seven-year-old Maria Cordero lived in San Juan, Puerto Rico, where she was born on June 12, 1932. This summer she was visiting her grandparents at their farm. Usually Maria stayed to swim in the river. She was a strong swimmer. But today she didn't care what she did. The word "divorce" was in her head. Her parents were getting a divorce.

After supper, everybody sat outside. Maria's grandfather, Vicente, played the violin. Other people who worked on the farm played the flute, or the cuatro, or the concertina. The songs of Puerto Rico were so sweet that Maria forgot about the divorce. Then the music stopped. Maria was filled with sadness again.

Her grandmother, Antonia, sat beside Maria. "You know, little one, you can choose."

"Choose what, Grandmama?"

"To be mostly happy or mostly sad," Grandmother answered.

"Not yet, Grandmama. Now I can only be sad," Maria said softly.

But, as time passed, Maria *was* able to feel happy. Her mother married again. Maria had no brothers or sisters. She lived with her mother and stepfather. She visited her grandparents every summer.

She liked working in her grandmother's flower garden. The roses smelled so sweet. The tree called the "Flamboyant Tree" was so beautiful.

The summer Maria was nine years old, she told her grandparents she was going to be a Girl Scout.

"I trust you will still behave as a lady should," Grandfather said.

"Oh, yes, Grandfather." Maria smiled to herself. Grandfather believed a lady should sit quietly, walk slowly, and never, never shout. But Maria raced the horse she rode at the farm. She hopped up the stairs two at a time. She whooped as she jumped the garden fence. Her grandfather said that was not "ladylike."

Maria asked her mother about it. "Of course you can race and jump and shout." Maria's mother smiled. "That does not mean you have to be rough and rude. You

can be strong and polite at the same time. Boys are expected to be both strong and polite. You can be too."

Strong and polite. Maria liked that. That was a good way to be.

Being a Girl Scout was fun. At one meeting the girls gathered different kinds of leaves. Then they looked in books to find the name of the tree each leaf came from. Maria said it was like being a detective.

"And a scientist is like a detective too," the troop leader said. "First you get the evidence. Then you try to find out what it means."

Maria remembered how she used to give her stuffed animals "vaccinations" with her mother's hairpin. That was acting like a

scientist too. Maybe, she thought, I will grow up to be a scientist.

When Maria was 10 years old, her parents decided she would get a better education at boarding school. At first it was hard living away from home. Maria did not want to do school work. Then she remembered about choices. I can do nothing, or I can do my best, she thought. Maria was not a girl who thought doing nothing was much fun. So she made her choice. She began to enjoy her home-away-from home. Her favorite class was science.

Maria liked sports too. She played catcher on the school softball team, the "All Stars."

Maria left Puerto Rico when she was 15 years old to go to college in Nebraska. Now she had to speak English all the time. Nobody spoke Spanish.

At Christmastime, Maria tried to get a job as a salesclerk in a store. "You do not speak English very well," she was told. "Our customers will not understand you." Maria was given a job wrapping packages in a back room.

After her first day of work, Maria's fingers were swollen from twisting and pulling string. Her arms ached from lifting packages. And she knew she was not going to earn as much money as a salesclerk. Maria knew she had another choice to make.

"I'm going to learn to speak English as well as I speak Spanish," Maria wrote to her mother. "I will speak it as well as anyone." Maria took more English classes. Her English got better and better.

Maria decided to be a scientist. She asked a professor about the best classes to take. "Why take up a man's place in any class?" he asked. "You'll just get married and forget about science."

"Men get married and have careers," Maria said. "Why shouldn't I?" The professor just smiled.

When Maria left his office, she did not feel defeated. She felt more determined than ever to be a scientist.

Then a terrible thing happened. Some men from Puerto Rico shot at the President of the United States. The President was not hurt, and the men were captured. Because Maria was from Puerto Rico, some people did not speak to her. Even some of her professors treated her differently.

This makes no sense, Maria thought. If a few people from Nebraska did something wrong, other people would not hate everyone from Nebraska! Why are they turning against me?

It was another choice to make. She could give up and go home to Puerto Rico. Or she could stay, study hard, and become the best scientist she could be. Maria chose to stay.

Maria graduated from college and went to Fordham University. There she earned her doctorate in physiology. Physiology is the science of how the body works. The doctorate is the highest degree a scientist can earn.

One summer Maria took a vacation in Europe. Afterwards she sailed home on a big ocean liner. On the ship she met Anthony Hardy, an Englishman. He was coming to America to study.

Maria and Tony continued their friendship in America. It was

such a successful friendship that they decided to marry. Now they have two children, Rick and Marisa.

As she grew up, Marisa, Maria's daughter, liked to play baseball. She wanted to join Little League. No girls were on the team. Marisa decided that did not matter. What mattered was that she liked baseball and was good at it. She chose to try out for the team.

Marisa became the first girl to play in Little League baseball in her town. Marisa played shortstop. She was one of the best hitters on the team. Marisa and the boys got along fine. The next year, other girls joined the team.

Sometimes Maria and Marisa's brother, Rick, came to watch batting practice.

Dr. Maria Cordero Hardy is now a professor at Louisiana State University and Program Director of the Department of Medical Technology. She teaches students to be medical technologists. These are the people who do tests on the blood, tissue, and fluids of the human body. The tests are very important because they help tell if people are sick and what can be done to help them get well again. It is very important that the tests be done right.

Maria also does her own research on Vitamin E. Her research helps scientists understand how the vitamin works in the human body.

Dr. Maria Cordero Hardy is happy with her life and her work. She knows that the choices she made, even when she was a little girl, were very important.

"It's your choice to work to be what you want to be, or to give up," she says. "It's your choice to decide to have a career, or a family, or both.

"Sometimes choices are hard. But if you don't make your own choice, someone else may make it for you. Then the choice may not be what you really want.

"Don't ever forget," says Dr. Maria Cordero Hardy, "choices

are your chance to choose the kind of life you want to lead.''